A Little Drip of Paint

Jessie Zou

A Little Drip of Paint
Copyright © 2022 by Jessie Zou

All rights reserved. No part of this publication may be reproduced, distributed, or transmitted in any form or by any means, including photocopying, recording, or other electronic or mechanical methods, without the prior written permission of the author, except in the case of brief quotations embodied in critical reviews and certain other non-commercial uses permitted by copyright law.

Tellwell Talent
www.tellwell.ca

ISBN
978-0-2288-7777-6 (Hardcover)
978-0-2288-7776-9 (Paperback)

This is a drip of paint.

A little drip
of paint.

So little,
she is
never seen.

That made her feel lonely.

For her...

Everyone was too **BIG.**

She searched everywhere for a friend.

But nobody noticed her.

Until...

...She changed!

Size AND Shape.

And a friend appeared.

"Will you be my friend?" she asked.

"Sure!" said the pear.

Now she was
no longer
a drip of paint.

She was an APPLE.

www.ingramcontent.com/pod-product-compliance
Lightning Source LLC
LaVergne TN
LVHW071654060526
838200LV00029B/461